D1328277

Space Scientist
THE
SUN

Heather Couper and Nigel Henbest

Franklin Watts
London New York Toronto Sydney

Important warning

Never look at the Sun directly – even through dark film or tinted glass. The Sun is powerful and will damage your eyes. **Never** ever look at the Sun through a telescope or binoculars – you will be permanently blinded. The **only** safe way to view the Sun is by using the projection methods shown on pages 27 and 28.

© 1986 Franklin Watts Limited

First published in 1986 by
Franklin Watts Limited
12a Golden Square
London W1R 4BA

First published in the USA
by Franklin Watts Inc.
387 Park Avenue South
New York, N.Y. 10016

First published in Australia
by Franklin Watts
Australia
14 Mars Road
Lane Cove, NSW 2066

UK ISBN: 0 86313 269 3
US ISBN: 0-531-10055-3
Library of Congress
Catalog Card No:
85-51135

Illustrations by
Drawing Attention
Rhoda Burns
Rob Burns
Eagle Artists
Michael Roffe

Designed by
David Jefferis

Printed in Italy by
G. Canale & C. S.p.A. - Turin

Space Scientist
THE
SUN

Contents

Our local star

The Sun is an immense ball of glowing gases, so large that it's almost impossible for us to grasp its size. It is 1·4 million km (860,000 miles) across – over a hundred times wider than the Earth and big enough in volume to contain more than a million Earths. The Sun's surface is far hotter than we can imagine, too. It is so hot that any substance – even metal or rocks – would melt and boil away if we took it to the Sun. We can feel the Sun's immense heat on a summer's day even though we are 150 million km (93 million miles) away.

The Sun's gravity keeps the Earth in orbit around it, so we never stray from its warmth and light. For this reason the Sun is very special and very important to us.

But the Sun is actually a very ordinary star – no different from the thousands of stars that we see in the sky at night. The Sun only seems so big and bright because it's so near to us. In fact, some of the stars that we see in the night sky (like Rigel, in Orion) are much bigger, brighter and hotter than the Sun – but they are dimmed by their immense distances from us.

Most stars are smaller, cooler and dimmer than the Sun. If we orbited one of these stars, the Earth would be perpetually frozen. When we take a look at all the different types of star, it turns out that the Sun is a very average star – middling in size, brightness and temperature.

The Sun, along with all the other stars we see in the night sky, is part of a huge "star-island," or galaxy, that we call the Milky Way. This flattened group of 100 billion stars is shaped rather like a fried egg. The Sun is about two-thirds of the way from the center to the edge, some 30,000 light years from the middle of the Milky Way.

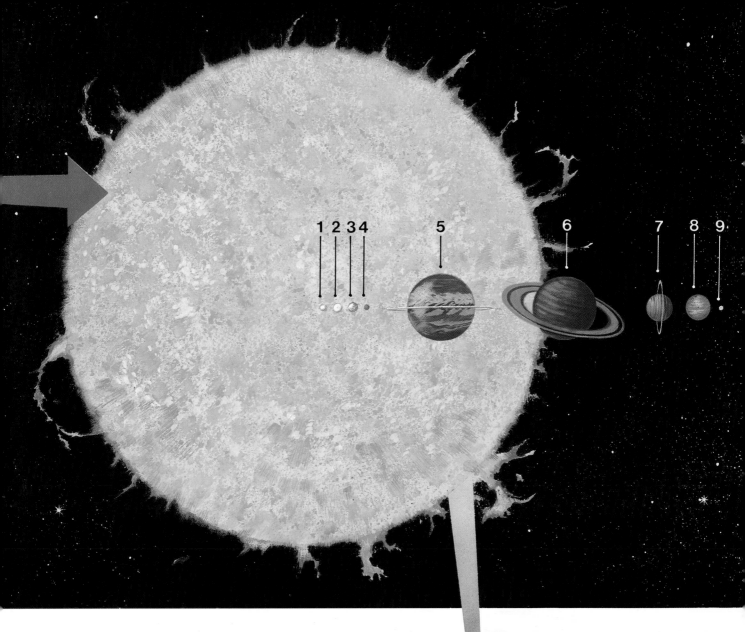

△ Our Sun is circled by a
family of nine planets. They
are:

1 Mercury
2 Venus
3 Earth
4 Mars
5 Jupiter
6 Saturn
7 Uranus
8 Neptune
9 Pluto

▷ The Sun's strong
gravitational pull holds the
planets in their orbits and
prevents them from flying
off into space. The Earth is
third in distance from the
Sun, at 150 million km (93
million miles), and it travels
round once in one year.

5

Day and night

The Sun provides the Earth with light. When the Sun is above the horizon, we have the brightness of daytime; and when it has set, we are plunged into the darkness of night.

If we look at the Earth from space, we can see that half the Earth is lit up by the Sun and is having daytime, while the other half is turned away and is experiencing night. Because the Earth spins round once every 24 hours, each part of its surface has a regular succession of day and night as it comes round to face the Sun and then moves on into the region that is in darkness.

The Earth's rotation means that the Sun appears to move across the sky during the day. The Sun seems to travel from east to west as the day progresses. We can tell the time approximately by noting where the Sun is in the sky.

In the morning the Sun is in the east; around midday it is halfway across the sky (to the south if you live in the northern hemisphere, but to the north if you are south of the equator); and in the evening the Sun is to the west. *Never* look directly at the Sun. Instead, look at the direction of the shadows thrown by sunlight.

As the Sun's light comes down through the Earth's atmosphere, the air scatters some of the blue light sideways. This light comes back to us from all directions and gives us our blue sky. The daytime sky is so bright that we cannot see any stars, although they are above the horizon by day as well as by night. The only time we can actually see stars during the day is when the Sun's light is blocked out by a total eclipse (*see* pages 16–17).

As the Earth turns, the Sun appears to

6

◁ The Sun lights up only half of the planet Earth, just as it illuminates only half the Moon. The lit side has "day;" the dark side has "night." The satellite relays TV signals both day and night.

△ At night we can tell that the Earth is rotating by watching the stars. They appear to move across the sky, circling the Pole Star (center). In this time-exposure photograph, the stars have left long trails.

drop towards the western horizon. As the Sun gets lower in the sky, sunlight must pass through more of the Earth's air. This removes more blue light, and the Sun turns red as it sets. It also seems bigger too. But this is only an illusion, caused by the fact that we are comparing the setting Sun with distant objects on the skyline. (Don't stare at the Sun even when it is setting – its heat can still damage your eyes.) If you are lucky, you may see a flash of green light just as the Sun disappears below the horizon.

As the Earth spins, the Sun appears overhead at different places around the world in succession. If the Sun is now halfway across the sky – midday – in London, it has only just risen in New York. Someone living in New York must wait another five hours until it is noon there, when the time in London will be 5.00 pm. To make sure that all countries have their own "noon" when the Sun is highest in the sky, the world is divided into time zones, and we must adjust our watches when we move from one time zone to another. (You will find a map of the world's time zones on page 30.)

▽ As the Sun sets, its light travels through curved layers of the Earth's atmosphere. This bends the light, and as a result the Sun seems to be slightly higher in the sky than it actually is. When the Sun appears to sit on the horizon, it is in fact just below it, but its image is bent upward by the air.

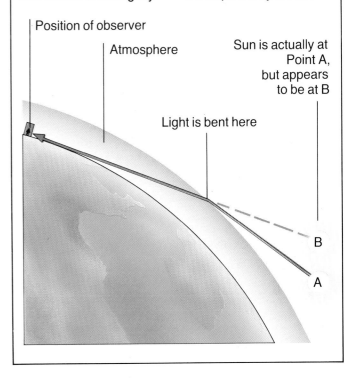

Position of observer

Atmosphere

Sun is actually at Point A, but appears to be at B

Light is bent here

B

A

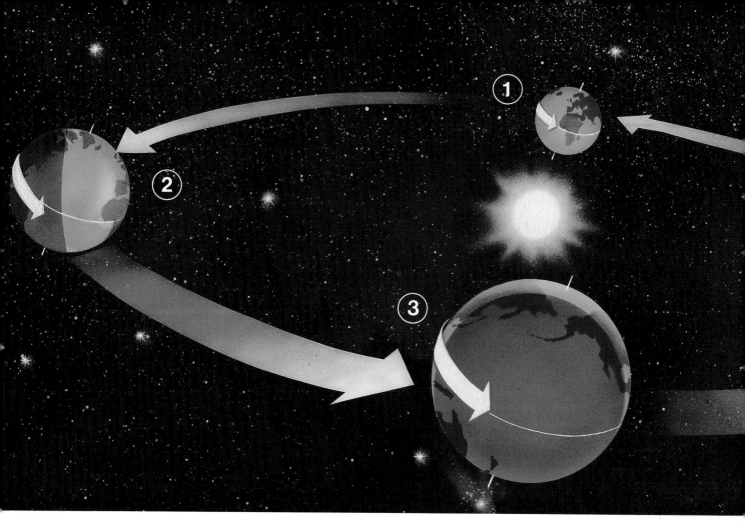

Summer and winter

We depend on the Sun to supply warmth to our planet: without it the Earth would be so cold that the air would freeze! Although some parts of the world are warmer than others, the Sun heats our planet to an average temperature of 15°C (59°F). This average temperature stays much the same as the Earth travels around the Sun, because its distance from the Sun remains more or less constant at 150 million km (93 million miles).

But during the year we get very big differences in temperature as the seasons progress: from the cold of winter to the heat of summer. In between are the less extreme seasons of spring and autumn.

The seasons are caused by a tilt in the Earth's axis, which means that each hemisphere is tipped toward the Sun for six months and away for six months. When our hemisphere is tilted toward the Sun, the Sun crosses high in the sky during the day. It stays up for a long time, giving us long days and short nights. This is summer. During summer days the Sun's heat is beating directly down on us, so we get the warmest weather of the year.

◁ From December to February the Earth's tilt means that sunlight is falling directly on to the southern hemisphere (**1**), delivering a lot of heat and giving summer conditions. But a similar amount of heat falling on the northern hemisphere (**2**) is spread out as it strikes the ground obliquely, and so provides less warmth.

1

2

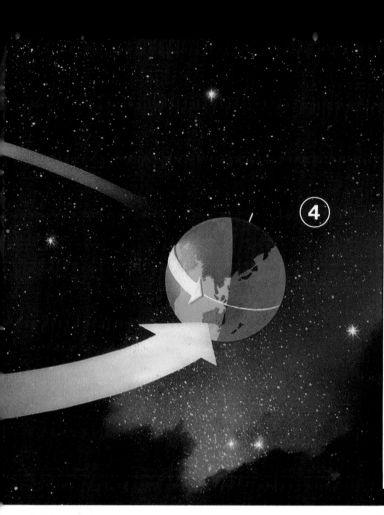

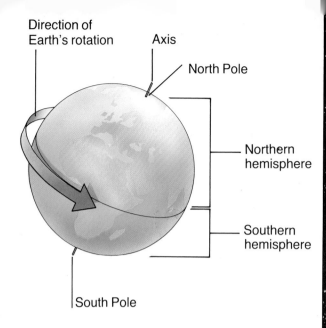

Direction of Earth's rotation

Axis

North Pole

Northern hemisphere

Southern hemisphere

South Pole

△ The Earth spins around an imaginary axis which runs between the North and South Poles. If we continue it out into space, it points in the direction of a star that we call the Pole Star, or North Star.

But the axis is not at right angles to the Earth's orbit around the Sun. It leans over at an angle of $23\frac{1}{2}°$. The North and South Poles are alternately tipped toward the Sun, so producing the seasons.

△ The northern and southern hemispheres have opposite seasons.
1 Northern spring: southern autumn.
2 Northern summer: southern winter.
3 Northern autumn: southern spring.
4 Northern winter: southern summer.

In the northern hemisphere this happens during June, July and August. The June solstice, June 21, is when the Sun is highest in the sky, although the weather is actually warmest a month later when land and sea have had a chance to warm up. At this time people in the southern hemisphere have winter, because they are tilted away from the Sun.

Six months later people in the north have winter. The Sun remains low in the sky during the day and delivers less warmth. But in the southern hemisphere it is the height of summer. On December 22 it is winter solstice in the northern hemisphere and summer solstice in the southern hemisphere. So people in the north associate Christmas Day (December 25) with snow and cold weather, while people in the southern hemisphere have Christmas lunch sunbathing on the beach.

△ The great stone monument Stonehenge in England was set up to mark the June solstice. As the seasons pass, the Sun appears to rise at different places along the horizon. In the northern hemisphere it rises in the southeast in winter; east in spring; and northeast in summer, reaching the most northerly point on about June 21. At Stonehenge you see the Sun rise over a special stone, the Heel Stone, on that day.

Inside the Sun

Although astronomers cannot see into the Sun, they can work out what it must be like by studying its surface and the amount of light and heat that it produces.

The Sun is made of gases throughout, mainly hydrogen and helium. The gas is at its most compressed, and its hottest, right at the very center, or core, of the Sun. This is where the Sun's tremendous output of light and heat is generated. The temperature here is about 14 million °C, and the gas is compressed to 12 times the density of lead.

Under these extreme conditions a process called nuclear fusion takes place. Atoms of hydrogen combine together to form atoms of helium. Each time this happens the atoms lose a small amount of their matter, which is turned into energy. The Sun's vast nuclear reactor converts some four million tons of matter into energy every second!

This nuclear energy produced at the Sun's hot core gradually seeps outward. At first the energy is in the form of radiation, like X rays and gamma rays. This inner region of the Sun is called the radiative zone. As the radiation travels outward, it meets a layer of gases in the convective zone. This layer becomes so hot that it begins to turn over, like milk in a pan that is about to boil. Eventually the heat travels to the surface, or photosphere, in streams of upward-flowing hot gases.

▷ **1** Core – the center of the Sun where energy is produced by nuclear reactions.
2 Radiative zone, where energy from the core travels outward in the form of radiation.
3 Convective zone. Huge convection currents stir up this outer layer of gas, carrying heat outward.
4 Photosphere (or sphere of light), the visible layer of the Sun.

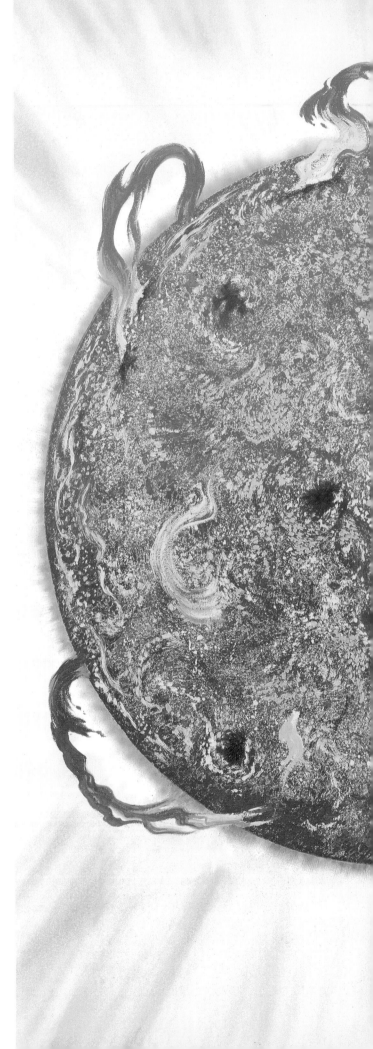

10

①

②

③

④

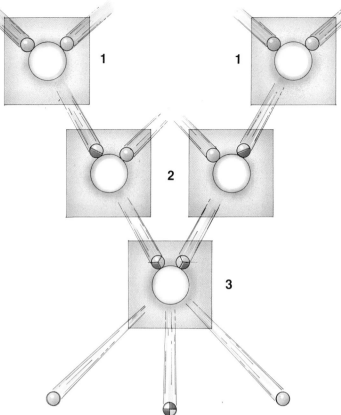

△ In the Sun's core a series of nuclear reactions converts hydrogen to helium, releasing energy at each stage.
1 Two hydrogen atoms combine to form deuterium ("heavy hydrogen").

2 Another hydrogen atom joins on to deuterium, to give a light variety of helium (helium-3).
3 Two helium-3 atoms collide, producing ordinary helium (helium-4) and liberating two hydrogens.

△ The power of the hydrogen bomb is caused by nuclear fusion reactions that are very similar to those in the Sun. Scientists are now trying to control nuclear fusion on Earth to provide cheap and abundant electricity from the hydrogen in sea water.

Sunspots and flares

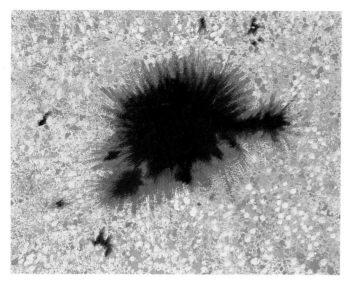

△ A close-up view of a sunspot shows that it has a very dark center (the umbra), surrounded by a brighter region called the penumbra. The spot's magnetic field spreads out from the umbra, causing the striped patterns in the penumbra.

The Sun's surface may at first seem to be rather smooth, featureless and uninteresting. But it does have its surprises: dark spots and occasional brilliant flares.

This visible layer, or photosphere, is not actually solid. It is the outer edge of the dense, opaque gases that make up the Sun. Powerful solar telescopes show that the photosphere is not smooth, but is speckled all over. This granulation is caused by the streams of gas rising and falling in the convective zone that lies immediately below.

Much more noticeable are the sunspots, small dark patches on the photosphere. If you make the Sun projector described on page 27, you should be able to see at least a couple of spots on any day (although the number does change markedly from year to year).

A sunspot is dark because it is cooler than the

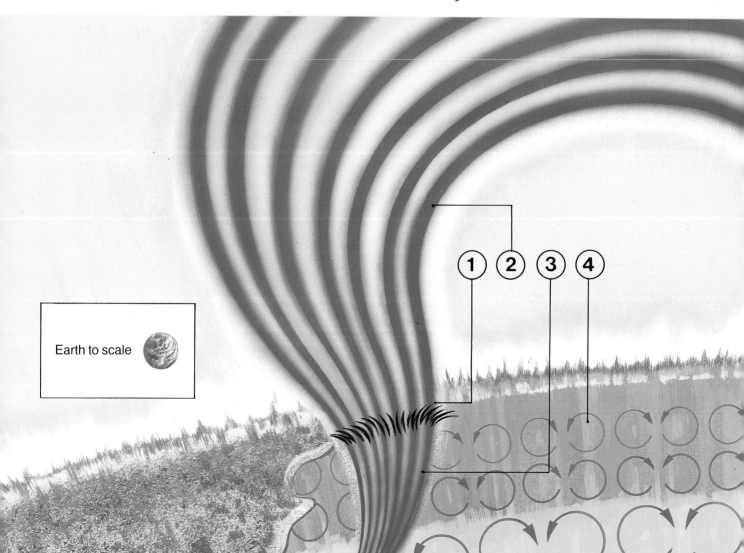

Earth to scale

① ② ③ ④

rest of the photosphere, at "only" 4000°C, compared with 5500°C elsewhere on the surface. A sunspot is caused by a magnetic field breaking through the Sun's surface. The strong magnetism dams back the flow of heat from the Sun's interior, causing the cool region that we see as a sunspot.

Sunspots often occur in pairs, at either end of a magnetic loop. A pair may develop into a more complex group, and then die away over a few weeks, as the magnetism grows stronger and then fades away. Changes in the magnetic field can also cause the brilliant outburst of a flare, a kind of violent sunstorm. A flare erupts with the energy of about a thousand million hydrogen bombs – but even so, astronomers need special instruments to see a flare against the brilliant photosphere.

By watching sunspots, astronomers have been able to discover how fast the Sun is turning. Relative to the stars, the Sun turns once in 25 days; but because the Earth is moving round the Sun, we see a spot come back to the same position after a slightly longer time – 27 days.

△ A flare is a sudden brilliant outburst of light from the Sun. Flares usually occur near sunspot groups. They seem to be magnetic explosions caused when two loops of magnetism touch – rather like an electrical short-circuit.

Inside a pair of sunspots

Sunspots (**1**) appear where the Sun's magnetic field (**2**) breaks through the surface. Normally the magnetic field (**3**) is buried deep inside the Sun. But over the years the Sun's spin twists it up like an elastic band, so that in places it breaks through the surface. The field "dams back" the normal convection ("boiling") motion (**4**) of the Sun's gases, which carries its energy to the surface. As a result, sunspot groups are cooler than the surrounding surface and appear much darker.

Earth
to
scale

The Sun's atmosphere

Above the photosphere we find the gases of the Sun's atmosphere stretching far into space. This very tenuous gas is invisible in ordinary telescopes, but astronomers have developed special telescopes to observe the ultraviolet radiation and X rays from the Sun's atmosphere. Some of these telescopes have been flown on the Skylab space station and the Solar Max satellite to enable scientists to get better views above the Earth's atmosphere.

The layer of gases immediately above the photosphere is called the chromosphere (or sphere of color). It glows a distinctive red. Unlike the Earth's atmosphere, which forms uniform layers around our planet, the chromosphere is irregular. Its gases are concentrated in certain regions, especially around sunspot groups, where they form into dense red clouds called plages.

△ X-ray pictures of the Sun, taken by astronauts aboard the Skylab space station, reveal the hot patchy gases making up the Sun's corona.

◁ Glowing gas clouds in the corona appear as beautiful red prominences. Some are supported by magnetic fields and can remain suspended for days of even weeks. Others are shorter-lived. They consist of gases that are flowing downwards from the corona towards the photosphere. The magnetic field can act like a catapult, flinging the gases outward.

▽ The Sun's atmosphere consists of tenuous gases beyond the photosphere (**1**). Both the inner atmosphere (**2**, chromosphere) and outer atmosphere (**3**, corona) are affected very strongly by the magnetic fields above sunspots (**4**). These cause narrow spicules (**5**); prominences (**6**); and long streamers (**7**) of gas that stretch out from the corona into interplanetary space.

In other places the gases of the chromosphere are concentrated into spicules, narrow "flames" that look like blades of red grass growing up from the photosphere.

Above the chromosphere stretches the even more tenuous corona. Its gases are extremely hot, at a temperature of over a million degrees. They are found mainly over sunspot regions, held there by magnetic fields looping up from the photosphere below. The corona's hot gases do not produce much light, but they do emit plenty of X rays, which have been detected and analyzed by X-ray telescopes.

Prominences are huge loops or arches of relatively cool gas that hang in the much hotter corona, supported by magnetic fields.

③

⑦

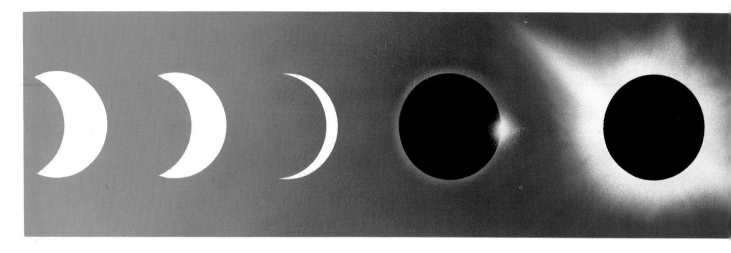

△ This sequence shows how the Moon moves in front of the Sun causing a total eclipse. During totality (center) the corona surrounds the dark Moon.

Eclipse!

We cannot usually see the Sun's atmosphere from the Earth's surface because its glowing gases are much fainter than the bright blue sky surrounding the Sun. Light from the Sun's brilliant surface, the photosphere, is scattered in the Earth's atmosphere, causing the blue sky. But if we could block off the photosphere's light with something above the Earth's atmosphere, the sky would go completely dark, and the chromosphere and the corona would be easily visible.

We do have something that will block off the Sun's light in this way. The Moon happens to be about the same apparent size as the Sun in the sky: although it is 400 times smaller, the Moon is also 400 times closer than the Sun. When the Moon moves right in front of the Sun, covering the photosphere, we have a total solar eclipse.

A total eclipse is an unforgettable experience. As the Sun is hidden, the whole sky goes dark. The stars come out, and animals and birds go to sleep, thinking that it is night. Although the Sun is blotted out, something wonderful seems

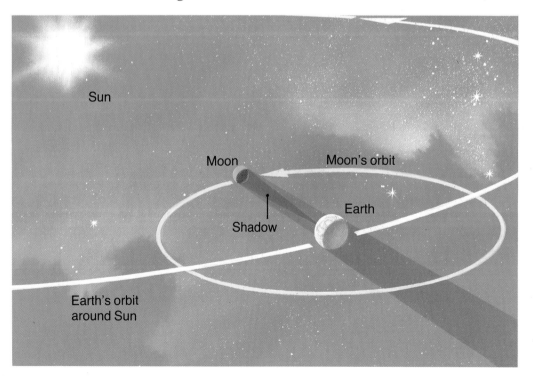

Sun

Moon

Moon's orbit

Shadow

Earth

Earth's orbit around Sun

◁ We see a solar eclipse when we happen to be in the Moon's shadow.

Because the Moon moves around the Earth every month, you might think that its shadow sweeps across the Earth each month, too. But in fact, the Moon's orbit is tilted, and in most months its shadow passes above or below our planet. Twice a year, however, the Moon's shadow can move across the Earth and cause an eclipse.

Even so, you must be in the right place to see it. The Moon's shadow is only 100 km (60 miles) wide as it crosses the Earth, so you must be within that narrow band to see a total eclipse.

to have taken its place. The red fringe of the chromosphere surrounds the dark Moon, and sometimes an enormous red prominence juts out from its edge.

The corona stretches outward, dimmer and dimmer, to several times the normal size of the Sun in the sky. Against the dark sky the pearly glow of the corona is easily visible to the eye, even though it is a million times fainter than the photosphere.

Then, in just a few minutes, it's over. As the Sun's bright photosphere begins to emerge from behind the Moon, the first brilliant point of light appears like a sparkling diamond on the red ring of the chromosphere. As more of the photosphere appears, the sky brightens, drowning the faint corona and the chromosphere – and daylight returns.

△ In a total eclipse (center) the Moon completely hides the photosphere. Much more common is a partial eclipse (left), where the Moon covers only part of it.

When the Moon is at the far point of its orbit, it appears too small to cover the whole photosphere, and we have an annular eclipse (right).

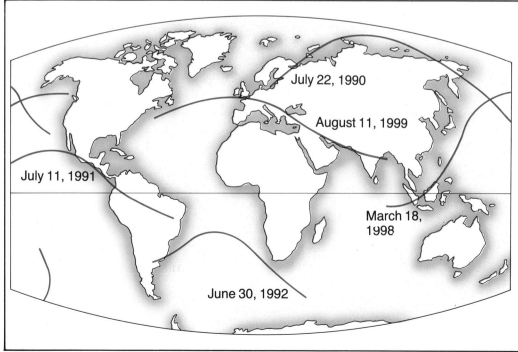

July 22, 1990

August 11, 1999

July 11, 1991

March 18, 1998

June 30, 1992

◁ The map shows where the Moon's shadow crosses the Earth (up to the year 1999). If you are exactly on one of these paths, you will see a total eclipse of the Sun on the date shown. If you are slightly away from an eclipse track, you will instead see a partial eclipse, but will not be able to see the chromosphere or corona of the Sun.

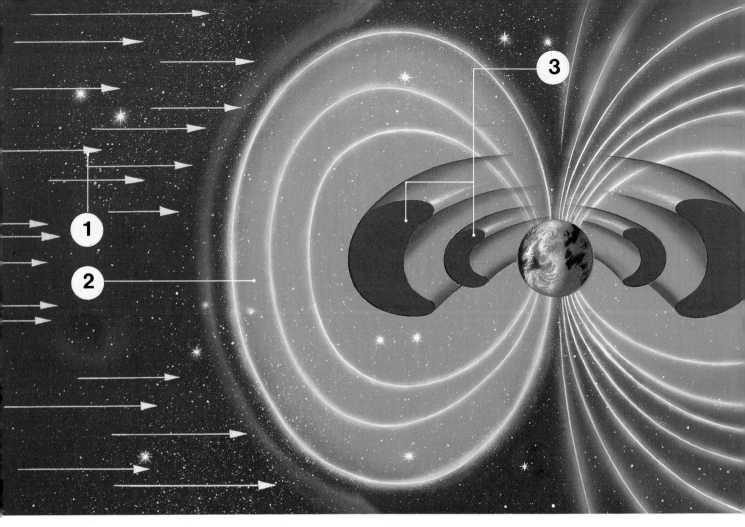

Winds from the Sun

The Sun's atmosphere does not have an outer edge. The gases of the corona stretch out through the Solar System, becoming more and more tenuous the farther they are from the Sun. The spacecraft Pioneer 10 has found that the solar atmosphere reaches out at least as far as the orbits of the outermost planets, Neptune and Pluto. This means that all the planets, including the Earth, are orbiting the Sun within its atmosphere.

These gases are not like an ordinary atmosphere, however. They are constantly moving away from the Sun, forming a "wind" that is forever blowing away from the Sun's surface and out past the planets. This solar wind carries away about a million tons of the Sun's matter every second – but the Sun is so vast that over its whole lifetime the solar wind will remove only one ten-thousandth of its matter.

As it sweeps past the Earth, the solar wind is blowing at a speed of about 1·6 million km/h (1 million mph), although when it is "gusty" it can travel twice as fast. The gas is very hot, at a temperature of about 100,000°C, but fortunately it is very tenuous, too, so the hot gas does not vaporize spacecraft in orbit around the Earth!

Most of the atoms in the solar wind are split up into their constituent particles – electrons and nuclei. These electrically charged particles are affected by magnetic fields, and as the solar wind passes the Earth, our planet's magnetic fields acts as a shield for the Earth. The solar wind has to sweep around the region of the Earth's magnetism (the magnetosphere), like the water in a river flowing past the solid piers of a bridge. On the far side of the Earth the wind stretches the Earth's magnetism out into a long "tail."

Van Allen belts

The Earth's magnetosphere helps to protect life on the Earth, because the high-speed electrically charged particles in the solar wind could damage living cells if they hit the Earth directly. But a few of these particles do creep into the magnetosphere, either above the North or South Poles or, coming the long way round, up the magnetotail. The Earth's magnetic field channels the particles down to the magnetic poles, where they hit the atmosphere and make it glow. This creates the spectacular colorful displays of aurorae – the Northern and Southern Lights – that we can see from regions near the Earth's poles.

The solar wind is far from constant: when there is a flare on the Sun, it creates a very powerful gust of solar wind. Such a gust takes three or four days to reach the Earth. When it arrives, we are treated to a spectacular display of aurorae. For any future astronauts in a spacecraft beyond our protective magnetosphere, a flare would be a very dangerous event, however. The intense gust of solar wind could damage body cells, leading to radiation sickness.

△ **1** Solar wind
2 Magnetosphere
3 Van Allen belts
4 Magnetotail
The Earth's magnetosphere protects us from the solar wind (blowing from the left here). The Van Allen belts are regions where solar wind particles are trapped above the equator.

△ An aurora is a glowing curtain of light, caused by particles from the solar wind hitting atoms of our atmosphere: oxygen atoms glow green, and nitrogen atoms produce a reddish light.

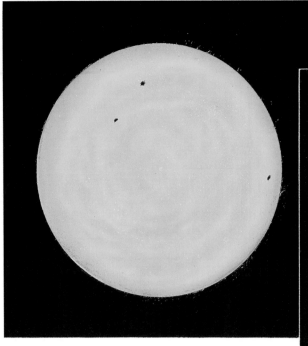

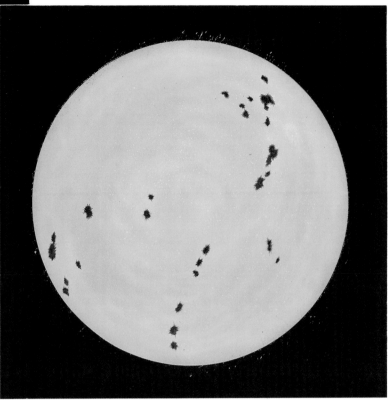

△ 1952 – few sunspots

▷ 1958 – lots of sunspots

The solar cycle

△ In 1952 (left) the Sun was at minimum and had only a few small sunspots. At sunspot maximum in 1958 (above) there were dozens of large spots.

The number of spots that we see on the Sun is not constant. In some years there are many; in other years relatively few. The number of spots comes and goes in a fairly regular cycle, reaching a maximum every 11 years.

At a time of sunspot minimum, as in 1975, the

Sun can be bare of spots altogether for weeks at a time. Then a few new spots begin to appear, well to the north and south of the Sun's equator. Over the succeeding years new spots appear in greater and greater numbers, closer and closer to the equator. By the time of sunspot maximum (which occurred in the last cycle in 1980) there may be a dozen large groups of spots on the Sun. Then the number of new spots begins to die away again as the Sun heads back toward sunspot minimum.

The appearance of sunspots is due to a cycle of magnetic activity within the Sun. The build-up of magnetism may be due to the Sun's rotation, which can twist up the magnetism inside its gases. Once the magnetism has broken through the surface, the loops of strong magnetic field can meet up in the Sun's atmosphere, where they short-circuit each

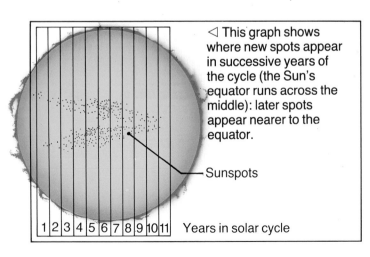

◁ This graph shows where new spots appear in successive years of the cycle (the Sun's equator runs across the middle): later spots appear nearer to the equator.

— Sunspots

1 2 3 4 5 6 7 8 9 10 11   Years in solar cycle

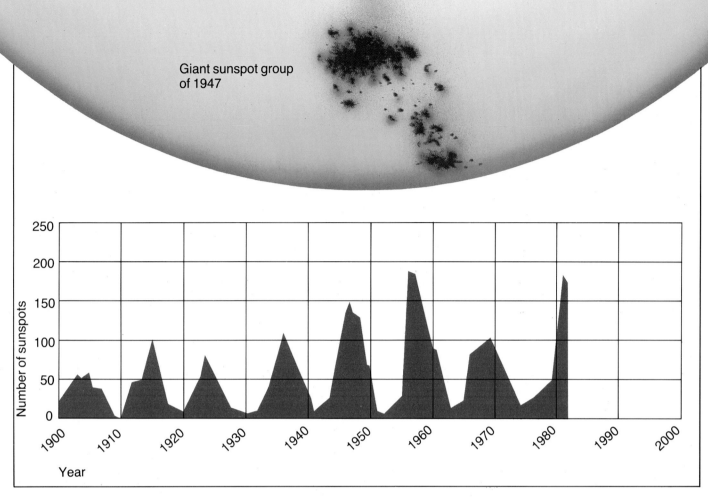

Giant sunspot group
of 1947

Number of sunspots

250
200
150
100
50
0

1900 1910 1920 1930 1940 1950 1960 1970 1980 1990 2000

Year

△ This graph shows the number of sunspots seen in each year since 1900. The number clearly goes up and down in a cycle of about 11 years. But the cycles are not identical. Some astronomers think that the number of sunspots at each maximum goes up and down with a cycle of 80 years.

▽ Some astronomers believe that sunspots affect our weather, causing an 11-year cycle in fruit harvests and in vintages of great wines.

other, producing flares. A flare reduces the strength of the magnetic field, and after a while the total magnetism of the Sun decreases again.

In each cycle the Sun's magnetism changes over. If in the last cycle the leading spot (the one in front as the Sun turns) of each pair was a magnetic "north pole," the leading spot in the next cycle will be a "south pole." So the Sun has to go through a period of 22 years before it returns to the same state of magnetism.

At times of sunspot maximum the Sun's activity reaches a peak in all ways: there are more flares, prominences and loops in the corona, and the solar wind is much stronger. Some scientists think that the changing strength of the solar wind can affect the Earth's atmosphere, making our weather change from good to bad, and back again, over a period of 11 years.

Birth and death

△ The Sun was born in a great gas cloud, like the Orion Nebula (above left). In its old age the Sun will swell to become a red giant (above). Seen here from Earth, from the bed of an ocean that has boiled dry, the Sun's surface is so close that its heat has driven off the air, making the sky black.

The Sun was formed about 5 billion years ago from a huge cloud of gas called a nebula. In the center of the cloud the gas drew together into a few dense clumps, and each of the clumps then shrank in size, pulled in by its own gravity. When the center of a clump became hot enough, nuclear reactions began, and the clump became a star that we call the Sun.

The gases swirling around the young Sun contained large amounts of solid dust particles. These gradually formed into the planets, including the Earth.

▷ The life-cycle of the Sun:
1 Nebula.
2 Young star.
3 The Sun today.
4 Red giant.
5 Planetary nebula is expelled.
6 White dwarf.
7 The Sun fades and cools, becoming a dark star or "black dwarf."

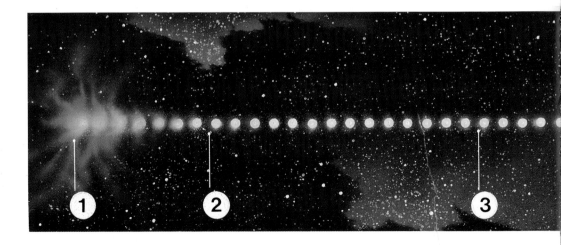

The Sun is now a middle-aged star, about half way through its life. In about 5 billion years time the center of the Sun will run out of the hydrogen gas that powers its nuclear reactions. The "ash" of helium from the nuclear reactions will then form into a small dense core at the Sun's heart.

When this happens, the Sun's outer layers of gas will swell up to compensate, and the Sun will grow to a hundred times its present size. Its surface will cool down, to glow a dull red color. The Sun will then be a red giant star.

The outer layers of a red giant are not stable, however. They pulsate in and out; and eventually the Sun will puff off its outer gases in a ring-like cloud called a planetary nebula.

Left behind will be the Sun's core, now exposed as a tiny, brilliant and very hot star called a white dwarf. The white dwarf will be very dense, and no larger than the Earth. But it will have no supplies of energy. Like an ember on a fire, it will gradually cool down, and eventually become a dark star invisible except at very close quarters.

Mysteries of the Sun

Although the Sun is right on our doorstep in the Universe, and is the star we can study best, it still has mysteries that leave astronomers puzzled. Here are some.

Frontier of the Sun's empire

How far does the Sun's influence reach? The most distant planet, Pluto, can travel out to a point 49 times further from the Sun than the Earth's orbit. But the Sun's gravity may hold sway much farther. Comets seem to come in from a great cloud known as the Oort cloud, which extends one thousand times further out than Pluto – almost a quarter of the way to the nearest star.

Some astronomers have recently questioned the existence of the huge Oort cloud, however. They think that the Sun picks up comets as it passes through dense clouds of gas in space.

A deadly companion?

Most stars have one or more companion stars, and the Sun is unusual in being alone. But is it? Several American astronomers believe that the Sun has a dark companion star which they call Nemesis.

They think that Nemesis goes around the Sun once in 26 million years. At its closest to the Sun, it would pass through the Oort cloud, dislodging some of its comets. These comets could fall into the inner part of the Solar System, possibly hitting the Earth and causing planet-wide devastation. These scientists think that this may be the cause of the eight "mass extinctions" of life on Earth (the most famous being the death of the dinosaurs) which seem to recur every 26 million years. Many astronomers are now looking for Nemesis to see if it does exist.

![Diagram showing Oort cloud surrounding the Solar System]

Oort cloud   Solar System

△ The Oort cloud is supposed to consist of billions of icy fragments which grow into comets when they approach the Sun. But astronomers still dispute whether the Sun could actually keep hold over such an extended empire.

▷ About 65 million years ago the great dinosaurs were all wiped out. Certain elements in the rocks of that period suggest that the Earth was hit by comets at about the same time. Were these comets shaken from the Oort cloud by a companion star?

The big chill

Although sunspots come and go every 11 years, there was a time in the late 17th century when astronomers saw no sunspots for 70 years. At the same time Europe experienced a series of extremely cold winters – a mini Ice Age when the Thames froze over, and Londoners held Ice Fairs on the river. Was this just coincidence, or did the lack of sunspots somehow cause this spell of severe cold?

The missing neutrinos

The nuclear reactions within the Sun that turn hydrogen into helium should also produce a lot of particles called neutrinos. Astronomers in the United States have set up a "neutrino telescope" to catch some of these elusive particles; but they have found only one-third as many as they expected.

What is wrong with our ideas of how the Sun shines? The simplest answer is that the Sun's core is slightly cooler than astronomers had previously thought; but if that is the case, the Sun should look rather dimmer than it does. So far, astronomers are still baffled.

△ A "neutrino telescope" is just a huge tank filled with a chemical similar to cleaning fluid! A neutrino will convert chlorine in the fluid into argon; scientists can then count the argon atoms. This tank is in a gold mine, 1·6 km (1 mile) underground, where it is protected from other forms of radiation.

Make a sundial

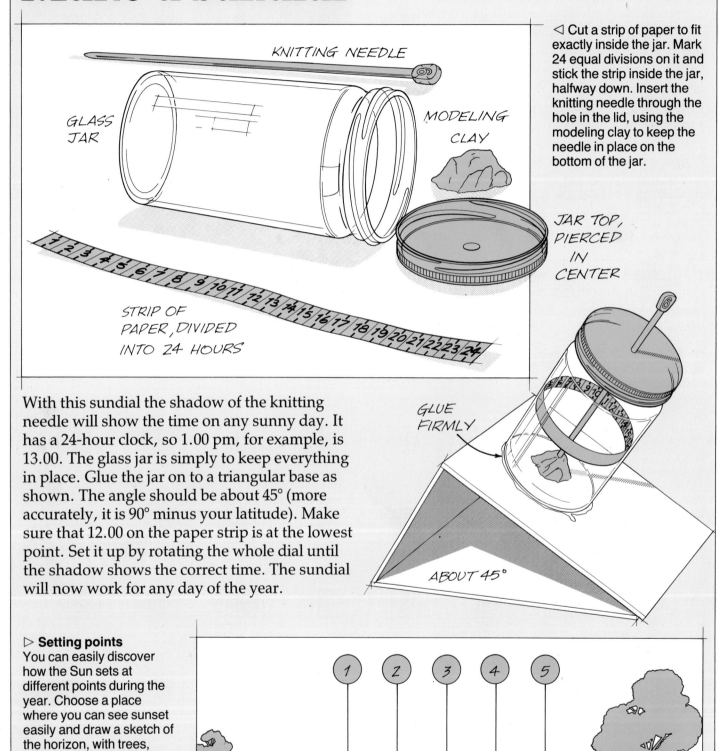

KNITTING NEEDLE

GLASS JAR

MODELING CLAY

JAR TOP, PIERCED IN CENTER

STRIP OF PAPER, DIVIDED INTO 24 HOURS

◁ Cut a strip of paper to fit exactly inside the jar. Mark 24 equal divisions on it and stick the strip inside the jar, halfway down. Insert the knitting needle through the hole in the lid, using the modeling clay to keep the needle in place on the bottom of the jar.

With this sundial the shadow of the knitting needle will show the time on any sunny day. It has a 24-hour clock, so 1.00 pm, for example, is 13.00. The glass jar is simply to keep everything in place. Glue the jar on to a triangular base as shown. The angle should be about 45° (more accurately, it is 90° minus your latitude). Make sure that 12.00 on the paper strip is at the lowest point. Set it up by rotating the whole dial until the shadow shows the correct time. The sundial will now work for any day of the year.

GLUE FIRMLY

ABOUT 45°

▷ **Setting points**
You can easily discover how the Sun sets at different points during the year. Choose a place where you can see sunset easily and draw a sketch of the horizon, with trees, houses, hills, and any other features. Mark where the Sun sets tonight. Continue marking the position of sunset once a week for several months.

1 2 3 4 5

Project the Sun

The only safe way to observe the Sun is to project its image on to a piece of white card, using some kind of telescope. Ordinary binoculars will do very well, but cover one eyepiece so that you only get a single image. This projector will easily show you sunspots.

WARNING

Never look directly at the Sun through a telescope or binoculars. Its intense heat and light can blind you.

▷ Attach a small piece of card to cover one eyepiece of the binoculars. Prop the binoculars in a window as shown, using the curtains to darken the room. Swivel the binoculars until sunlight shines through the eyepiece. *Do not put your eyes near the eyepiece at any time.* Focus the binoculars, moving the eyepiece quite far out, until the Sun's image is in focus on the large piece of white card.

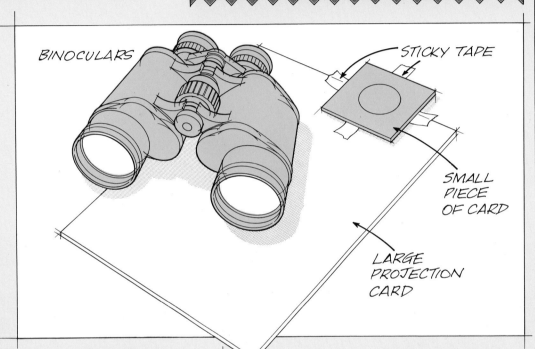

BINOCULARS

STICKY TAPE

SMALL PIECE OF CARD

LARGE PROJECTION CARD

PROP UP SECURELY

DON'T FORGET TO COVER ONE EYEPIECE WITH SMALL PIECE OF CARD

▽ Put a piece of tracing paper over the white card and mark the positions of the sunspots. Record the date, too. If you mark the spots for several days, you will notice how they move across as the Sun rotates on its axis.

Observe an eclipse

You will be very lucky if you see a total eclipse from where you live, but partial eclipses are quite common. Do not look directly at the Sun during a partial eclipse, however; enough hot surface is still exposed to cause blindness. This pinhole eclipse-viewer is the safe answer.

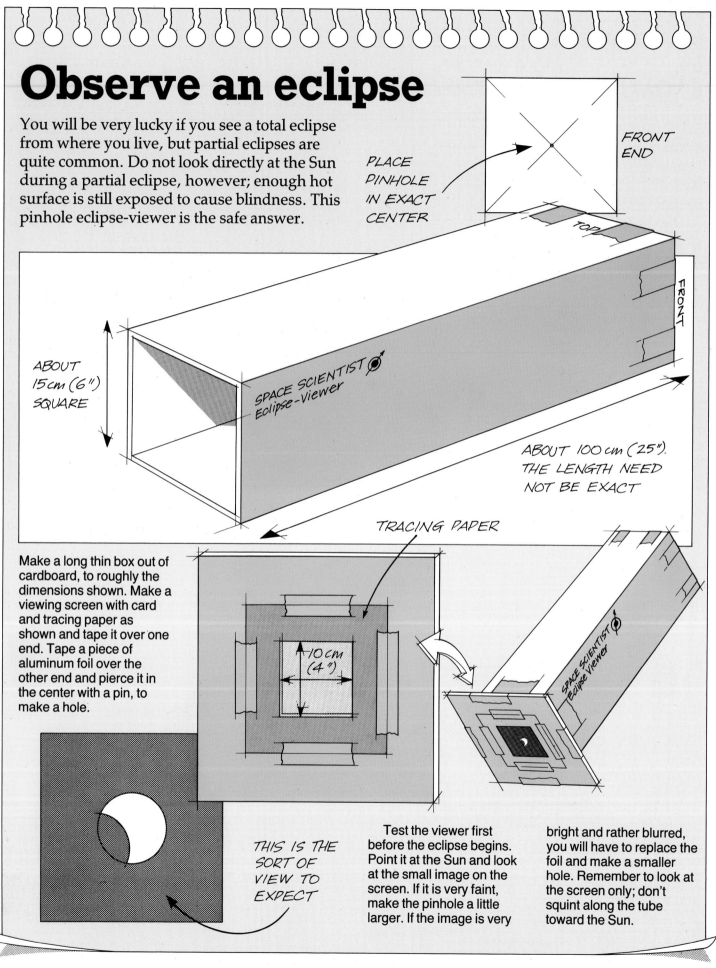

PLACE PINHOLE IN EXACT CENTER

FRONT END

TOP

FRONT

SPACE SCIENTIST Eclipse-Viewer

ABOUT 15cm (6") SQUARE

ABOUT 100 cm (25"). THE LENGTH NEED NOT BE EXACT

TRACING PAPER

10 CM (4")

Make a long thin box out of cardboard, to roughly the dimensions shown. Make a viewing screen with card and tracing paper as shown and tape it over one end. Tape a piece of aluminum foil over the other end and pierce it in the center with a pin, to make a hole.

SPACE SCIENTIST Eclipse Viewer

THIS IS THE SORT OF VIEW TO EXPECT

Test the viewer first before the eclipse begins. Point it at the Sun and look at the small image on the screen. If it is very faint, make the pinhole a little larger. If the image is very bright and rather blurred, you will have to replace the foil and make a smaller hole. Remember to look at the screen only; don't squint along the tube toward the Sun.

28

The aurorae

The aurorae – Northern and Southern Lights –
are caused by the Sun, even though we see
them at night. At sunspot maximum (the next is
due in 1991) and after a major flare, the aurorae
are more common and brighter than usual. But
you have to be somewhere far from the equator
to see the aurorae well. You can photograph
aurorae with an ordinary camera if you use fast
film (ISO 200 or more). Support the camera
firmly on a wall or a tripod and take several
exposures ranging from 15 seconds to one
minute.

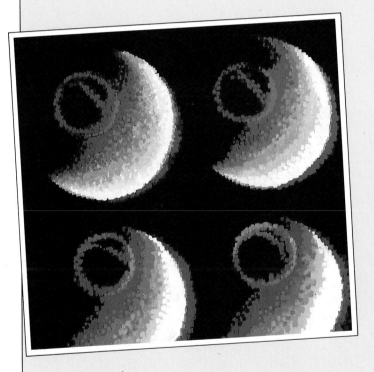

◁ Viewed from a satellite,
the aurorae form a
complete circle around the
Earth's magnetic pole,
where the magnetism
directs solar wind down on
to the atmosphere.

▽ Solar wind particles can
creep through Earth's
protective magnetic shield
in two ways – either up the
long magnetotail, or
through the two polar
cusps that lie above the
magnetic poles.

△ Photographs can show
the beautiful colors in the
aurora, and the stars
beyond. But the fine details
in the rapidly shifting
curtains will be blurred
because of the long
exposure time needed to
record the faint auroral
light.

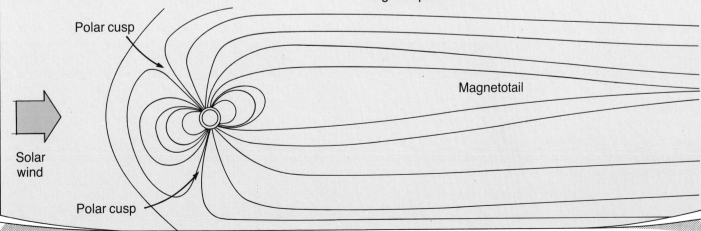

Polar cusp

Magnetotail

Solar
wind

Polar cusp

Glossary

Black dwarf A star at the very end of its life after it has cooled down from being a white dwarf. The Sun will end as a black dwarf.

Chromosphere The lower layer of the Sun's atmosphere, just above the photosphere.

Comet A small icy body that comes in from the outer Solar System.

Convective zone The uppermost region within the Sun where energy is transported upward to the photosphere by moving streams of gas.

Core The very central region of the Sun where energy is produced by nuclear reactions.

Corona The outer layer of the Sun's atmosphere. It consists mainly of gases trapped in magnetic fields above sunspots: elsewhere the gases escape freely from the chromosphere to the solar wind.

Eclipse (of the Sun) When the Sun's surface is hidden by the Moon. If the Moon completely obscures the Sun, the eclipse is total; if it covers only part of the Sun, we see a partial eclipse. An annular eclipse occurs when the Moon is at its far point; the Moon appears too small to completely block out the Sun and it leaves a ring (annulus) of photosphere showing around the dark Moon.

Flare A sudden brightening of a small region of the Sun's surface. A flare produces all kinds of radiation, including radio waves and X rays, and it ejects high-speed particles into the solar wind.

Helium The second lightest chemical element, and the second most common substance in the Sun after hydrogen.

Hydrogen The lightest element. It is by far the commonest substance in the Sun and in the Universe as a whole.

Magnetosphere The region of magnetic field around a planet. It is confined in a "magnetic bubble" by the solar wind flying past.

Magnetotail The region of a planet's magnetosphere away from the Sun, drawn out into an elongated shape by the solar wind.

Nebula A cloud of gas in interstellar space, where stars are being born.

Nuclear reaction A reaction between the centers of atoms (their nuclei). A nuclear reaction produces a great amount of energy and changes one kind of element into another.

Oort cloud A vast cloud of comets, stretching almost a million million km from the Sun. It forms a "reservoir" of comets in "deep freeze;" occasionally one comes toward the Sun and appears as a comet in our skies.

Penumbra The outer part of a sunspot, not as dark as the central umbra.

Photosphere The visible "surface" of the Sun.

Plage A dense red cloud of chromospheric gases found near sunspots.

Planetary nebula A misleading name for the gases ejected by a giant red star.

Polar cusp A narrow corridor just above each of the Earth's magnetic poles which allows some solar wind particles down into the atmosphere.

Prominence A cloud of dense gas hanging in the corona. Prominences can take distinctive shapes, including arches and loops.

Radiative zone The inner region of the Sun, where energy from the core travels outward in the form of radiation, especially X rays.

Red giant A very large and cool star. All stars become red giants toward the end of their lives: the Sun will "go red giant" in 5 billion years' time.

Solar cycle A period of 11 years (or so) over which all forms of solar activity – sunspots, flares, prominences – reach a maximum and then fade away. It is a more general term for the "sunspot cycle."

Solar wind The constant stream of gas that heads away from the Sun and out through the Solar System. It is the outermost part of the Sun's atmosphere.

Spicule A narrow vertical spike of gas in the chromosphere.

Time zones

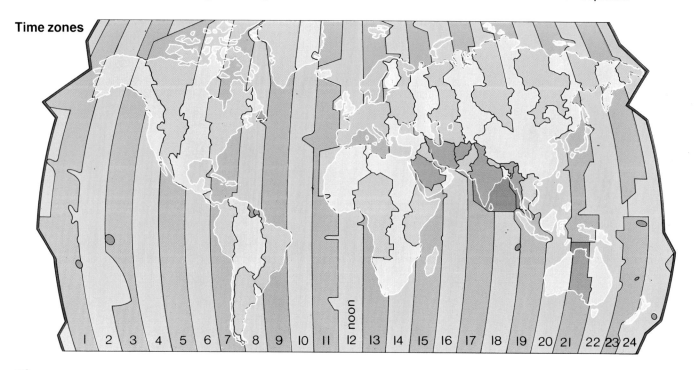

| I | 2 | 3 | 4 | 5 | 6 | 7 | 8 | 9 | 10 | 11 | 12 noon | 13 | 14 | 15 | 16 | 17 | 18 | 19 | 20 | 21 | 22 | 23 | 24 |

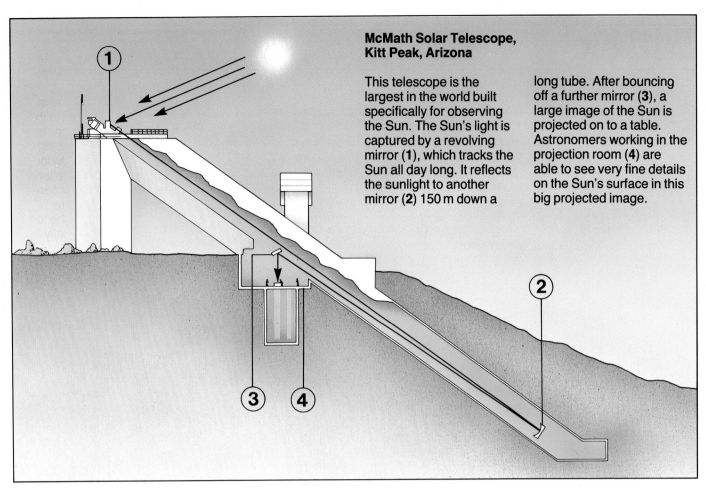

McMath Solar Telescope, Kitt Peak, Arizona

This telescope is the largest in the world built specifically for observing the Sun. The Sun's light is captured by a revolving mirror (**1**), which tracks the Sun all day long. It reflects the sunlight to another mirror (**2**) 150 m down a long tube. After bouncing off a further mirror (**3**), a large image of the Sun is projected on to a table. Astronomers working in the projection room (**4**) are able to see very fine details on the Sun's surface in this big projected image.

Sunspot A dark, cool patch on the Sun's surface, caused by a concentration of magnetic field.

Sunspot cycle The increase and decrease of sunspots every 11 years; part of the solar cycle.

Time zone A region of the Earth where all the clocks show the same time. The Earth is divided into 24 main time zones, each occupying about 15° of longitude. Some countries cover several time zones.

Umbra The very dark central part of a sunspot.

Van Allen belts Regions within the Earth's magnetosphere where solar wind particles are trapped above the equator.

White dwarf A very small, dense star. It is the core of a red giant, left exposed when the giant star sheds its outer gases. A white dwarf has no source of nuclear energy: it gradually fades and cools, to become a black dwarf.

Finding out more

The Sun is a typical star – with the added advantage that you can observe it during the day too. One of the best ways to follow up an interest in the Sun, the stars and stargazing is to join an astronomical society.

Find out if there is a club in your home town by writing to The Astronomical League, c/o Carole J. Beaman, Editor, *The Reflector*, 6804 Alvina Road, Rockford, Illinois, 61103. *The Reflector* keeps you up-to-date with news of local society events. In Canada the main astronomical association is the Royal Astronomical Society of Canada, 124 Merton Street, Toronto, Ontario, Canada M4S 2Z2. This society is aimed at people who have some knowledge of astronomy, so you might feel happier joining a local club first of all.

Once you've joined up, you'll find plenty to do – like making new friends, going to meetings, having star parties, constructing telescopes, or visiting places of astronomical interest.

The US has several observatories especially devoted to looking at our nearest star. The most famous is Sacramento Peak Observatory, located at Sunspot in southern New Mexico, which has specialized telescopes for studying the Sun.

At Kitt Peak National Observatory, near Tucson, Arizona, is the McMath Solar Telescope – the biggest in the world. Astronomers there can study an image of the Sun over three quarters of a meter across. There is an excellent Visitor Center at the site.

One of the most unusually sited solar observatories lies in the center of Big Bear Lake in southern California. The water prevents the build-up of turbulence from the Sun's heat at midday and the pictures taken there are very steady.

As well as the observatories, many planetariums and science centers feature the Sun's disk projected on to a table or a screen. Check with your local center.

Index